Y0-CKL-415

A Gift For:

Quin

From:

Aunt Shelly

Come near to God, and God will come near to you.
- JAMES 4:8

Copyright © 2018 Hallmark Licensing, LLC

Published by Hallmark Gift Books,
a division of Hallmark Cards, Inc.,
Kansas City, MO 64141
Visit us on the Web at Hallmark.com.

All scriptures, unless otherwise noted, are taken
from the International Children's Bible®. Copyright
© 1986, 1988, 1999 by Thomas Nelson.
Used by permission. All rights reserved.

Scripture from the New Century Version®.
Copyright © 2005 by Thomas Nelson, Inc.
Used by permission. All rights reserved.

Scriptures marked NIV are taken from the Holy Bible, New International Version®,
NIV®. Copyright © 1973, 1978, 1984, 2011 by Biblica, Inc.® Used by permission
of Zondervan. All rights reserved worldwide. www.zondervan.com. The "NIV" and
"New International Version" are trademarks registered in the United States Patent
and Trademark Office by Biblica, Inc.®

Scripture quotations are taken from the Holy Bible, New Living Translation,
copyright © 1996, 2004, 2007 by Tyndale House Foundation. Used by permission
of Tyndale House Publishers, Inc., Carol Stream, Illinois 60188. All rights reserved.

All rights reserved. No part of this publication
may be reproduced, transmitted, or stored in any
form or by any means without the prior written
permission of the publisher.

Editorial Director: Delia Berrigan
Editor: Kim Schworm Acosta
Art Director: Chris Opheim
Designer: Scott Swanson
Production Designer: Dan Horton

ISBN: 978-1-63059-702-3
BOK1341

Made in China
1018

DEVOTIONS FOR GIRLS

GROWING WITH GOD

Hallmark

BY DIANA MANNING   ILLUSTRATED BY CHARLIE HADLEY

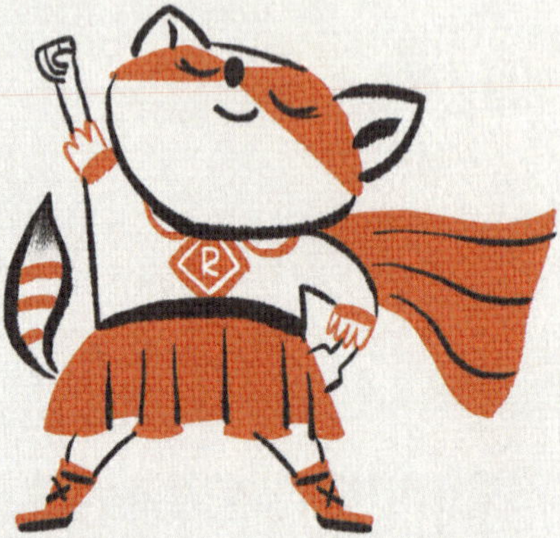

GOD MADE YOU

I praise you because you made me
in an amazing and wonderful way.
- PSALM 139:14 NCV

Did you know that God Himself made you? He created all the things about you that make you the girl you are—your eyes, your smile, the color of your hair, and the way you talk and think. That makes you His child . . . and you will always be one of His favorite creations!

I like to think God must have smiled when He created me, His child!

GOD KNOWS YOU

"Lord, you know everyone's heart."
- ACTS 1:24 NIV

Because God made you, He knows everything about you—what's inside your heart, what makes you happy or sad, and all the things you need in life. Nobody else knows you quite the way He does!

God, I feel so close to You, for no one knows me like You do!

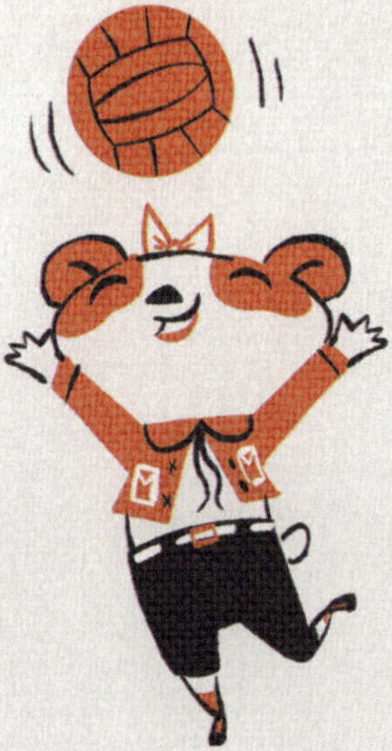

GOD LOVES YOU

"God loved the world so much that he gave his one and only Son so that whoever believes in him may not be lost, but have eternal life."

- JOHN 3:16 NCV

Good news! God has shown us how much He loves us by sending us His Son, Jesus, to be our Savior. Jesus is God's way of putting His arms of great big love around us. What a special gift!

I'm so glad God sent His Son to show His love to everyone!

GOD LISTENS

But God has listened. He has heard my prayer.
- PSALM 66:19

Are there things on your heart that you want to share with God? He's always listening, you know. He loves it when you come to Him with a prayer. Praying is the very best way to feel close to God, and you can be sure He hears you—because you're someone very precious to Him!

It feels so good to know God's there and listening to my every prayer.

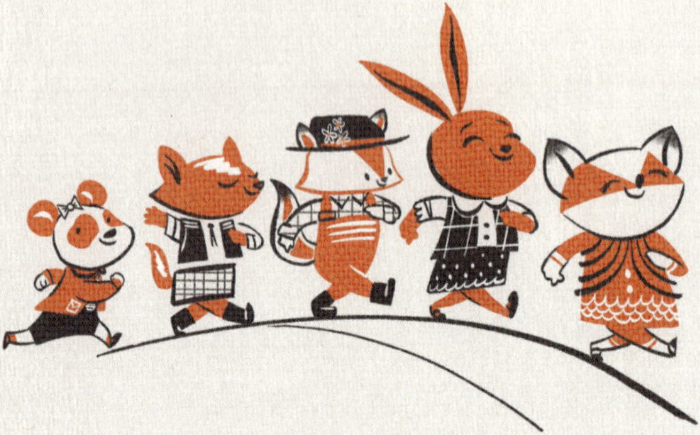

JESUS LOVES CHILDREN

But Jesus said, "Let the little children come to me. Don't stop them, because the kingdom of heaven belongs to people who are like these children."

- MATTHEW 19:14

Just because you're little doesn't mean you're not important to Jesus. He has said He loves little children, and wants to bless them in a special way! He even thinks big people could learn a lot from them. And best of all, he wants you to come to Him and get to know Him better . . . because He loves you!

I may be little, but I know that Jesus always loves me so.

GOD'S WORD HELPS US KNOW HIM

Your word is a lamp to guide
my feet and a light for my path.
- **PSALM 119:105 NLT**

Have you ever used a flashlight to help you see where you were going? God's word, the Bible, is kind of like that flashlight. It helps us take the right paths in life, and shows us how to live and the right things to do. It tells us what God has done and all the ways He's taken care of His family . . . that's us!

The Bible helps me know God's way and how to walk with Him each day.

FRIENDS ARE GOD'S GIFT

A friend loves at all times.
- **PROVERBS 17:17 NIV**

God gives us friends who care about us . . . friends to talk with and play with and have fun with. Everyone needs friends! But God wants us to know that the best way to MAKE a friend is to BE a friend. Can you be a good friend to someone today?

Of all the blessings that He sends, I'm thankful that God gave us friends!

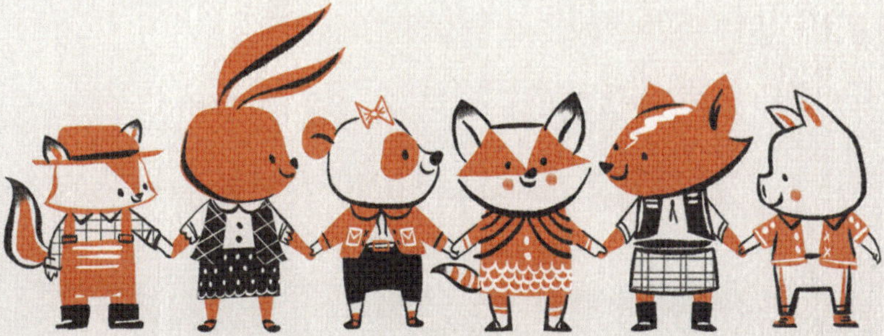

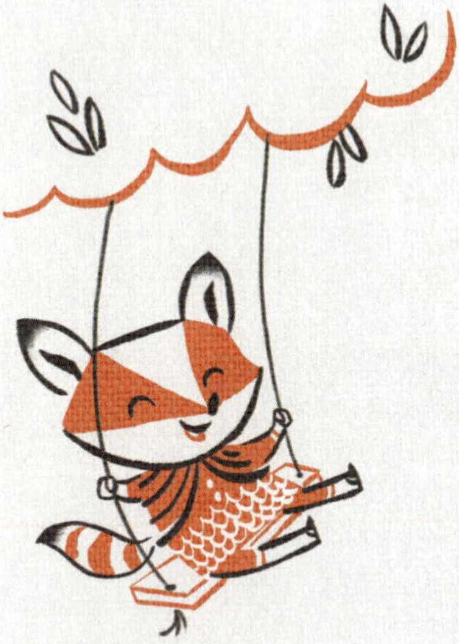

GOD IS WITH YOU ALWAYS

"You can be sure that I will be with you always."
- **MATTHEW 28:20**

Do you ever wonder if God is with you when it's dark? Is He with you when you're scared? Or when you're laughing and playing? The answer is YES! He's promised to be with you ALL the time! And that's a really good feeling.

Wherever I may be,
God, you're always here with me!

BE KIND

Be kind and compassionate to one another.
- EPHESIANS 4:32 NIV

God wants us to be kind to one another. That's the way the world works best. Even just the small things we do can bring a big smile to someone's face. It's one more way God takes good care of us . . . through each other!

Being kind and helping out is what God's love is all about!

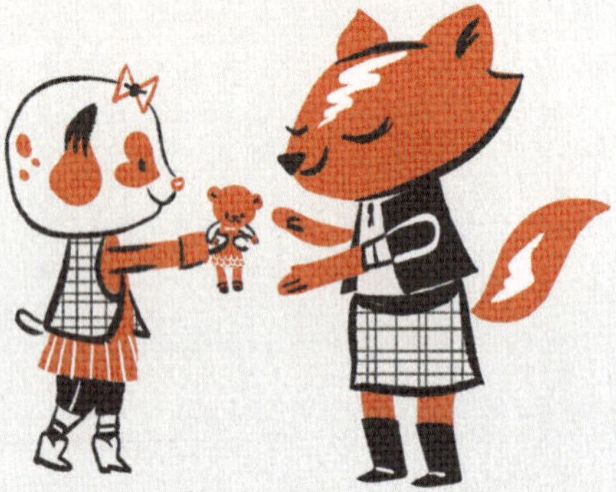

REMEMBER THE GOLDEN RULE

"Do for other people what you
want them to do for you."

- LUKE 6:31

Thinking about other people's feelings is important. How would we feel if we were in their place? Jesus said we should remember that—especially when we decide how we treat others. Sometimes that means sharing with someone.

I like it when people are nice to me,
so nice to others is what I'll be!

GIVE YOUR WORRIES TO GOD

Don't worry about anything; instead, pray about everything. Tell God what you need, and thank him for all he has done.

- PHILIPPIANS 4:6 NLT

It's so good to know we can bring all our worries to God. He's big enough to handle anything! He wants us to talk about things with Him in prayer because He cares about everything that happens to us.

Worries seem to fade away when I turn to God and pray.

JESUS IS OUR GOOD SHEPHERD

"I am the good shepherd; I know my sheep and my sheep know me."

- JOHN 10:14 NIV

Did you know that you're one of Jesus' little lambs? He told us in the Bible that He is our shepherd. That means He watches over you and takes care of you the way a shepherd does with his sheep. That means you're very special to Him, too!

Wherever I wander, wherever I walk, Jesus is with me—I'm one of His flock!

GIVE THANKS

Always give thanks to God the Father for everything, in the name of our Lord Jesus Christ.
- **EPHESIANS 5:20**

Everyone likes to hear a "thank you" when they give a gift or do something nice for someone. And nobody deserves more "thank yous" than God, who gives us everything we need! We say "thank you" for our food before meals . . . but how many other things can we thank Him for?

I thank you, God, every day
for all good things You send my way!

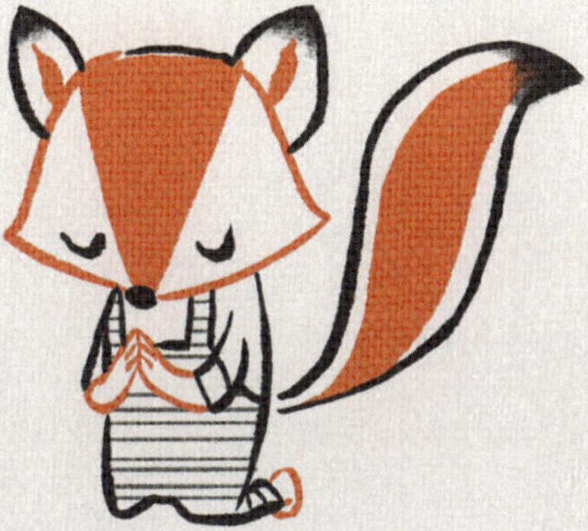

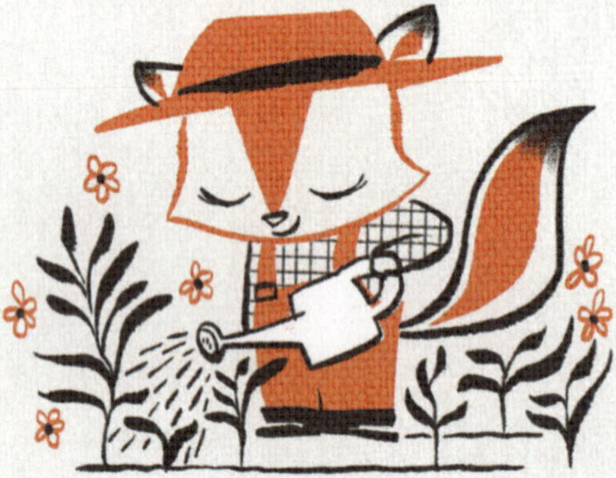

WE SEE GOD IN HIS CREATION

Everything that God made is good.
- 1 TIMOTHY 4:4

We see God's work all around us in the beautiful things that He has made. He wants us to enjoy His amazing creation, because He loves us so much. What an awesome God He is to create such wonders!

From rainbows and robins to the sun on my face, God made the world such a beautiful place!

LISTEN TO YOUR PARENTS

Children, obey your parents in everything,
for this pleases the Lord.

- COLOSSIANS 3:20 NIV

God gave you parents for a reason—they're the ones who know what's best for you. They love you and take care of you. So if you listen to them and do what they ask, you show that you love them, too! And that's what being a family is all about.

I'm glad my parents love me like they do— dear God, please help me show I love them, too!

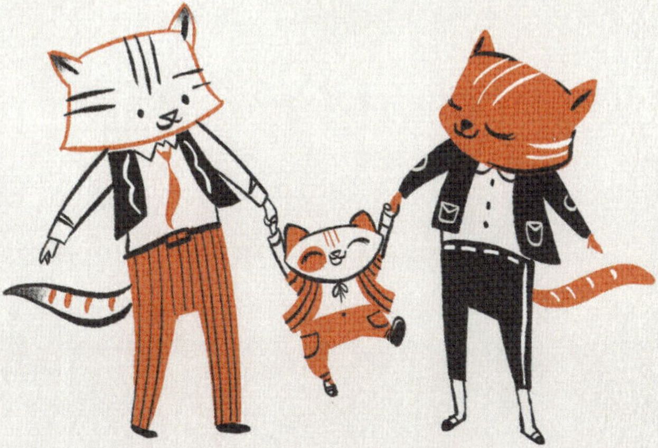

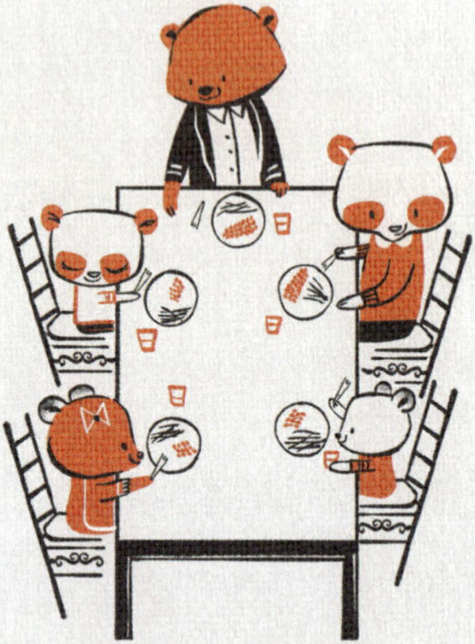

GOD GIVES US ALL WE NEED

My God will use his wonderful riches in Christ Jesus to give you everything you need.
- **PHILIPPIANS 4:19**

Sometimes we don't have everything we *want*. But God makes sure we have everything we *need*, because He's our Heavenly Father and He takes good care of us. He knows you need a place to live, and food and clothes and a family to love you. He knows just what you need—even before you ask Him!

---

*God sends all I need each day—
His love is never far away!*

FORGIVE OTHERS

Forgive each other just as
God forgave you in Christ.

- EPHESIANS 4:32

When people hurt our feelings or make us mad, God wants us to forgive them. And God shows us the way by forgiving us when we do wrong, too. Forgiveness isn't always easy, but talk it over with God. He'll help you let go of angry feelings.

Forgiving isn't quite as hard to do when we remember we're forgiven, too.

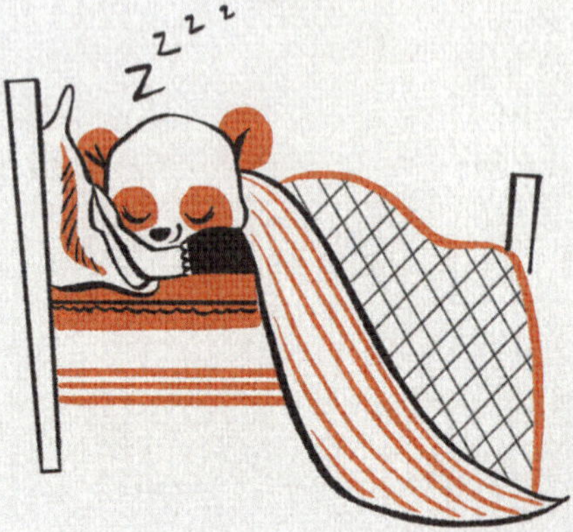
Zzzz

GOD IS THERE WHILE YOU SLEEP

I go to bed and sleep in peace.
Lord, only you keep me safe.

- PSALM 4:8

When you close your eyes at night to go to sleep, God still sees you and watches over you. In fact, He never takes His eyes off you, because you're that special to Him! He helps you feel sleepy and snug in your bed. He gives you the gift of rest.

God watches over me each night and always keeps me in His sight.

GOD LOVES TO HEAR YOU SING

I will sing the Lord's praise,
for he has been good to me.
- PSALM 13:6 NIV

Making music is another way we can feel close to God. He loves to hear the sound of your happy heart singing songs to Him! Can you think of a song you've learned about God? You can sing it any time and know it makes God smile!

I love to sing to God above
and praise His name for His great love!

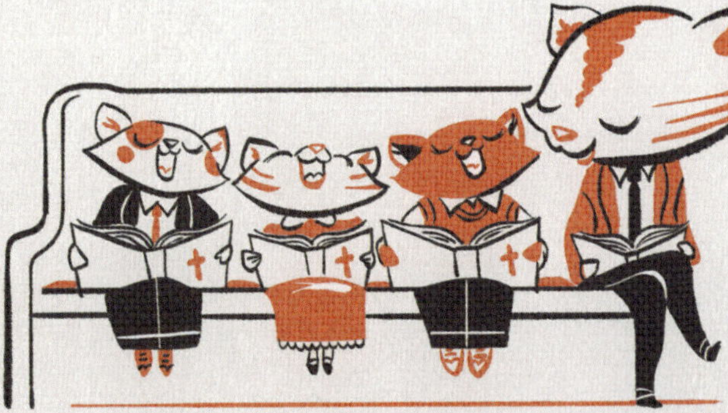

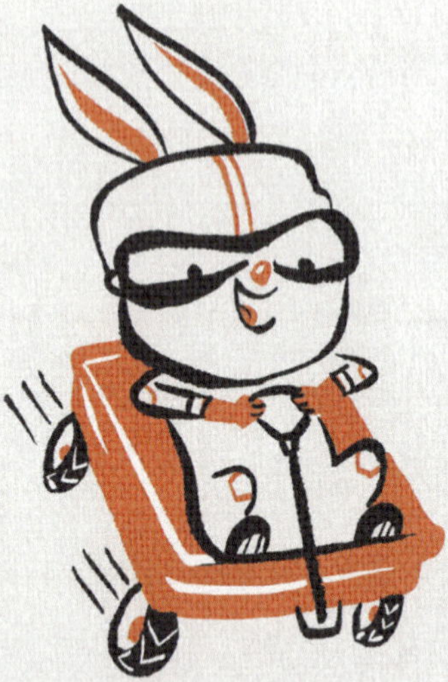

BE JOYFUL!

Be full of joy in the Lord always.
- PHILIPPIANS 4:4

Jesus wants us to be happy. He tells us in the Bible that He is joyful, too! His joy comes from staying close to God, His Father. He gives us lots to be happy about, because He loves us. But no matter what is happening in our day, when we stay close to God, we can always have His joy in our hearts.

I love to laugh and run and play—
God fills my heart with joy each day!

HAVE PATIENCE

A wise person is patient.
- PROVERBS 19:11

It's hard to wait for what we want. But God tells us we need to be patient. Some things simply take time. And God will help you to learn patience if you ask Him. He will help you to be patient with other people, too . . . just like they are patient with you sometimes!

*If I am patient, I'll be blessed—
God hears my prayers and knows what's best!*

GOD KEEPS YOU STRONG

He will make you strong.
He will support you and keep you from falling.
- **1 PETER 5:10**

Some days you may feel like you're too little to do the things you want to do. But you're stronger than you think, because you have God to help you! Nobody is stronger than He is, and He's always on your side. Day by day, you're growing stronger and stronger in the Lord!

God says He will make me strong and be with me my whole life long!

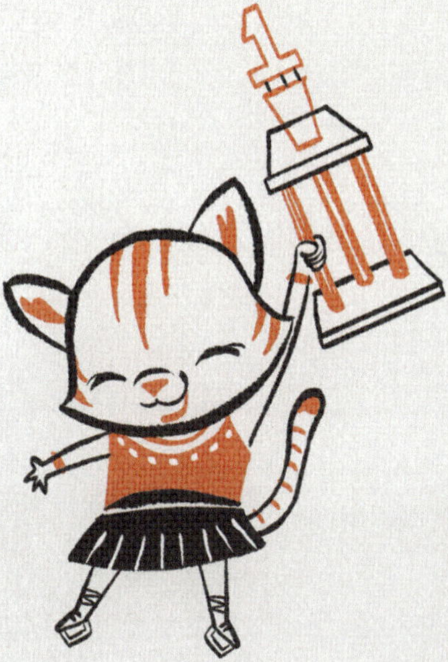

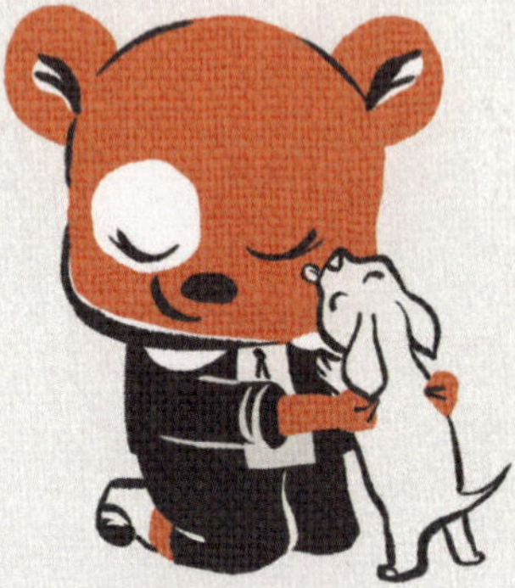

SERVE OTHERS WITH LOVE

So be good servants and use your
gifts to serve each other.

- 1 PETER 4:10

Jesus had so much love in His heart, He lived His life serving others. He gave them food to eat, washed their feet, and spent time being their friend. He told us in the Bible that He wants us to be like Him. That's why serving is so important. Can you think of a way you can serve somebody today?

Serving others helps to share God's love with people everywhere!

HAVE FAITH

Faith means being sure of the things we hope for. And faith means knowing that something is real even if we do not see it.

- HEBREWS 11:1

We know God is real even though we cannot see Him. That is called "faith." And when you read Bible stories and spend time with God in prayer, your faith will grow! Jesus said that God can do big things through our faith. He said all things are possible, if we believe. What a wonderful promise He gave us!

---

*I have faith in God above—
I know He's real and feel His love!*

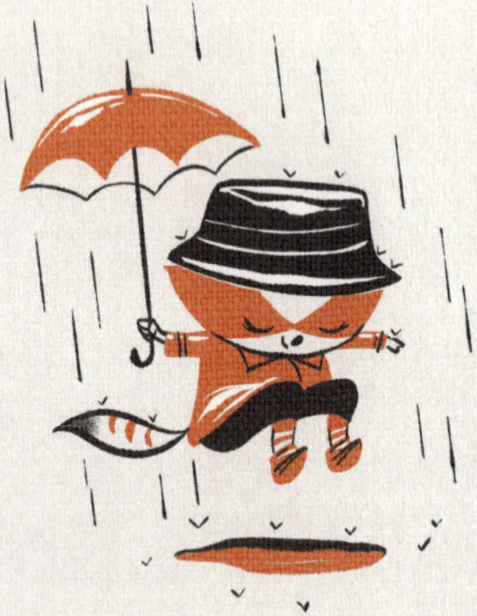

BE A LIGHT

"You are the light that gives light to the world."
- MATTHEW 5:14

When you have God's love on the inside, it shines out for all the world to see! That's what Jesus meant when He said we should be a light for other people. You can be a good example for others and share God's love with them. That way others can come to know God, too!

I'll be a light so others see God's goodness shining out through me!

GOD HAS A PLAN FOR YOU

"I have good plans for you . . . I plan to give you hope and a good future."
- **JEREMIAH 29:11**

Do you ever think about what you'll be when you grow up? A doctor? A teacher? A baker, maybe? God has had some great plans for you ever since you were born! And even someday when you're a grown-up woman, He'll still be with you. He has a good life planned for you . . . because He loves you!

I can't wait to someday see the good things God has planned for me!

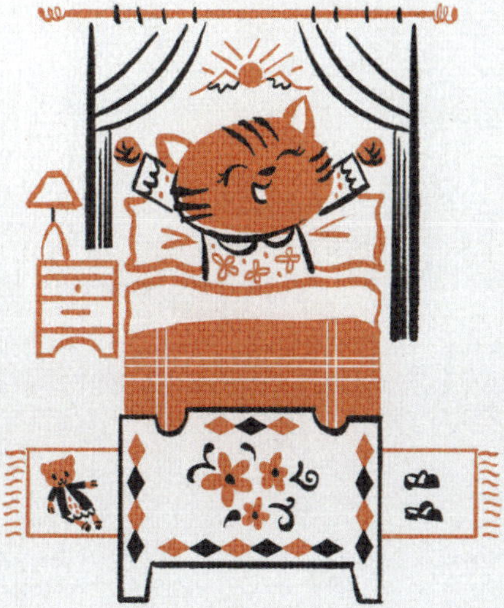

Did you enjoy these devotions?
We would love to hear from you.

Please write a review at Hallmark.com,
e-mail us at booknotes@hallmark.com,
or send your comments to:

Hallmark Book Feedback
P.O. Box 419034
Mail Drop 100
Kansas City, MO 64141

This book is dedicated to the Joy Team staff.

One key to success is to
surround yourself with wonderful people,
and I have certainly done that
with our staff.

Winning with Wisdom

Wisdom is the principal thing.
Therefore, get wisdom.

The Bible tells us, "Wise men store up knowledge..." (Proverbs 10:14 NKJV). Did you know the quality of your life is determined by the quality of your decisions, and the quality of your decisions is determined by the quality of information you "store" up? Therefore, if we truly desire a better quality of life, we must make better quality decisions with better quality information.

This little "nugget" style book is designed to invest in your storehouse of knowledge so you can eventually enjoy a better quality of life. As you peruse the pages of this book, don't be overwhelmed by the quantity of information, but rather focus in on the quality of change.

Remember this: invest in knowledge now, and it will compound in wisdom later!

You are not a loser; you are a "chooser"! *Winning with Wisdom* is designed to help you make your next right decision.

- JIM FREASE

INVEST IN
KNOWLEDGE NOW,
AND IT WILL
COMPOUND IN
WISDOM LATER.

WINNING WITH WISDOM

PEARLS OF WISDOM FOR YOUR NEXT RIGHT DECISION

VOLUME 2

Table of contents

LIFE CHOICES 10	VICTORY 46
FAMILY 86	FRIENDS 122
FINANCES 154	GOD'S LOVE 172

TODAY'S DECISIONS AFFECT

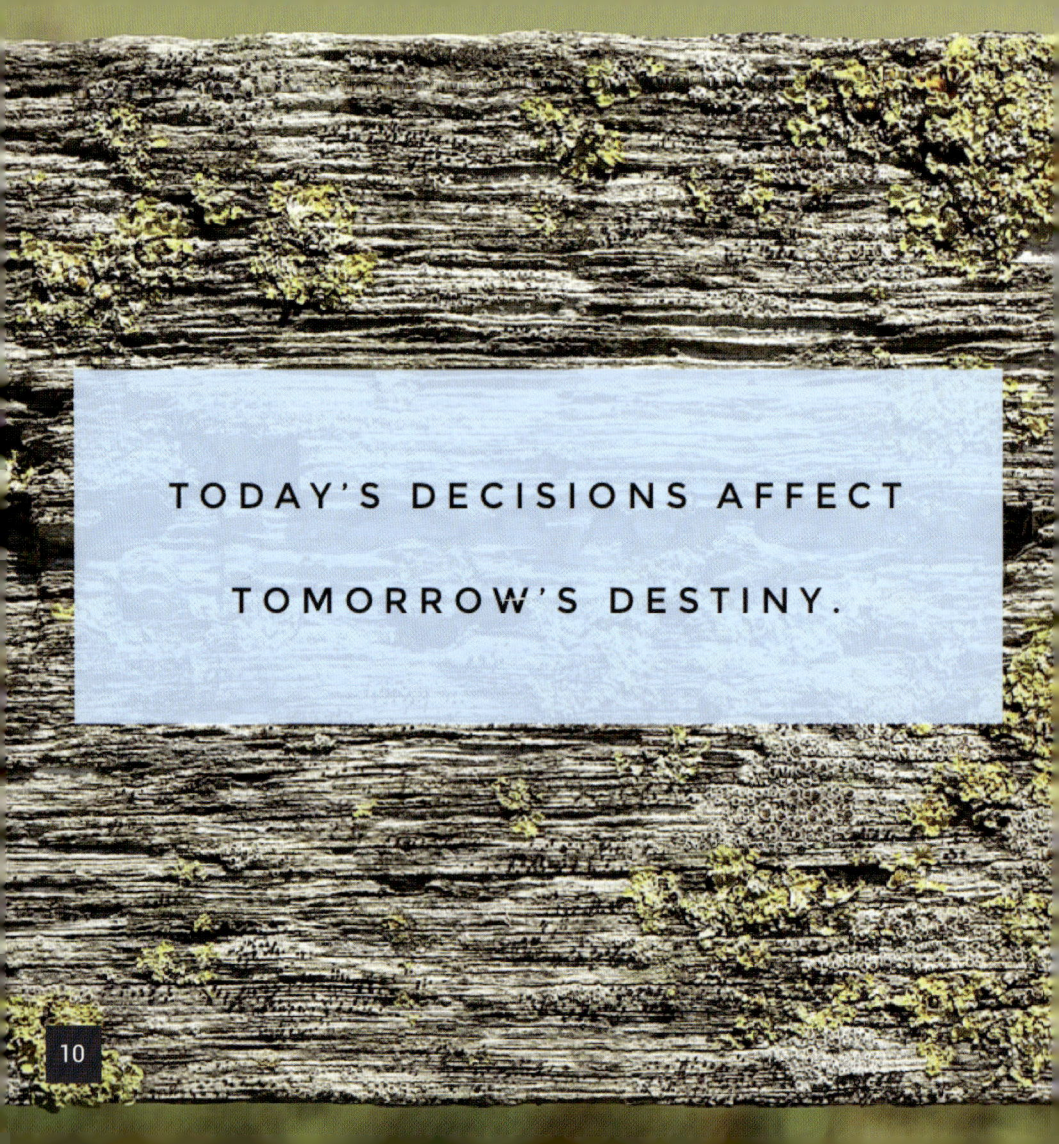

TOMORROW'S DESTINY.

LIFE CHOICES

LIFE CHOICES

Whatever is first in your life will determine your decisions.

Whatever is first in your life is set up to meet your needs.

in the beginning...
G O D

LIFE CHOICES

You will never change your life
until you change something you do daily.

Make daily decisions that inspire
a better way of living in others.

YESTERDAY IS HISTORY.

TOMORROW IS A MYSTERY.

TODAY IS A GIFT.

LIFE CHOICES

Commitment is not a one-time choice,
but a daily choice.

You choose your choices.
Your choices choose your consequences.

BE CONSISTENTLY
CONSISTENT

LIFE CHOICES

You were born for eternity.
Now, live for eternity.

Don't lower your expectations for Earth.
Simply raise your expectations for Heaven.

Are you goal-oriented or God-oriented?

LIFE CHOICES

Be courageous,
but not careless.

Cast away your care,
but not your responsibility.

COURAGE IS SIMPLY DOING IT AFRAID.

LIFE CHOICES

If you don't have a vision,
join with someone who does,
and yours will unfold.

As long as you think you can
handle something by yourself,
you will be limited by your own ability.

> YOU CAN'T DRIFT YOUR WAY TO SUCCESS. YOU HAVE TO DETERMINE YOUR WAY TO SUCCESS.

LIFE CHOICES

**Don't just work hard;
work smart.**

**If it's not broken,
improve it.**

LEARN TO SQUEEZE
EVERY BIT OF SEASONING
OUT OF EVERY SEASON.

LIFE CHOICES

Don't blend in.
Stand out!

Build on past successes and
learn from past failures,
but don't camp in either.

ALWAYS SEPARATE *who you are* FROM WHAT YOU DO.

LIFE CHOICES

We must make decisions that will create an awesome future instead of an acceptable present.

Never let your future be a period of time in which you regret not doing what you are not doing today.

WE MUST LEARN TO LIVE FOR ETERNITY AND NOT FOR THE NEXT WEEKEND!

LIFE CHOICES

If you don't overcome in life,
you'll be overwhelmed in life.

Some people are afraid to die.
Others are afraid to live.

IF YOU ARE AFRAID OF DYING, YOU WILL NEVER KNOW *how to live!*

LIFE CHOICES

As long as you continue
to be condemned
about what you have done,
you are doomed to repeat it.

Never let your tragedy
become your identity.

NEVER LET WHAT YOU DID YESTERDAY DETERMINE WHO YOU ARE TODAY

LIFE CHOICES

The cost of discipline is high,
but the cost of regret is higher.

Missed opportunities can bring
eternal regrets.

MANY TIMES,
WE WANT THE RESULTS OF CHANGE
WITHOUT BEING WILLING
TO PAY THE PRICE OF CHANGE.

LIFE CHOICES

The problem you hate
may be the problem
you were created to correct.

In every battle,
we must learn to pray the promise,
not the problem.

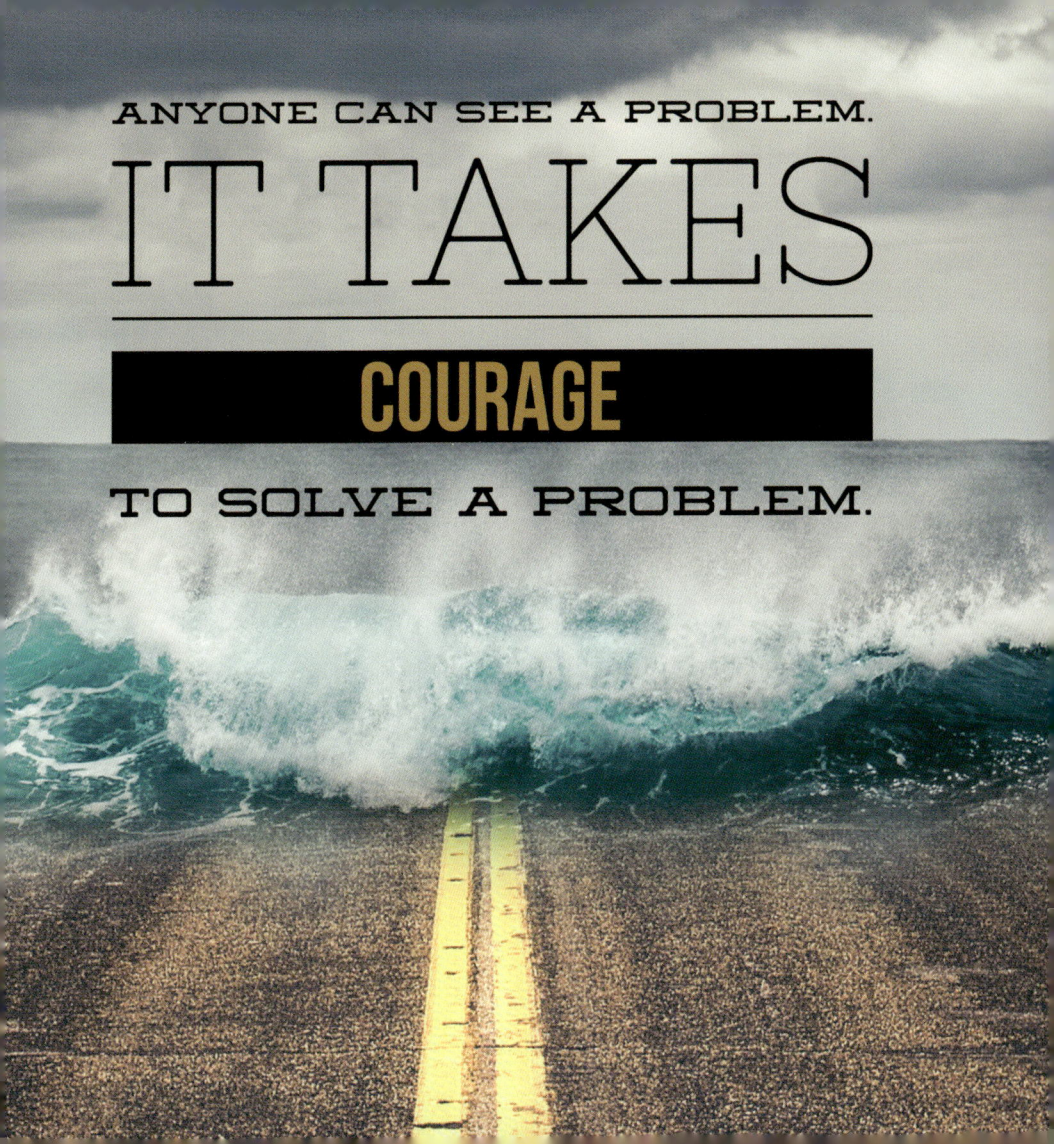

ANYONE CAN SEE A PROBLEM.
IT TAKES
COURAGE
TO SOLVE A PROBLEM.

LIFE CHOICES

Character is winning the battle between what you want to do and what you should do.

Discipline is the avenue through which destiny will travel.

DO THE RIGHT THING

WHEN YOU DON'T FEEL LIKE IT.

LIFE CHOICES

The root of procrastination
is either fear or laziness.
Take authority over it!

Time is not found; it's created.
Time is created based on priority.
Therefore, life is not about time management;
it's about priority management.

ARE YOU MANAGING LIFE
OR IS LIFE MANAGING YOU?

LIFE CHOICES

The longer you put something off,
the harder it becomes to do.

Patience is the ability to continue
to do the same things with
no apparent difference in circumstances.

DO NOT LET CIRCUMSTANCES ADJUST YOU.

ADJUST YOUR CIRCUMSTANCES.

LIFE CHOICES

Always look for silver linings
in clouds of crisis.

Believe you can do it.
God does!

GREAT CONFIDENCE IS A PREREQUISITE FOR GREAT ACCOMPLISHMENTS.

> TRUE POWER IS KNOWING WHAT TO DO IN ANY SITUATION TO BRING VICTORY.

VICTORY

VICTORY

All feelings come from thoughts.
All thoughts can be changed by words.

If you see and hear the same things,
you'll think the same thoughts
and stay the same person.

THINK LIKE A VICTOR. TALK LIKE A VICTOR.

VICTORY

The decisions you make,
the actions you take,
and the words you speak
are all seeds that will connect you to
or disconnect you from
a better tomorrow.

Make a quality decision
to not let your past control you.

MAKE DAILY DECISIONS THAT MATCH THE SIZE OF YOUR VISION.

VICTORY

Start small and simple.

God takes complex things
and makes them simple.
The devil takes simple things
and makes them complex.

SMALL

Is Not

a number.

small is

A MENTALITY.

VICTORY

When you eliminate excuses,
you begin on the road to excellence.

Intolerance of your present conditions
is the beginning of a better future.

DON'T GET BITTER.
GET BETTER!

VICTORY

Condemnation frustrates.
Conviction motivates.

Condemnation is the power to be chained.
Conviction is the power to be changed.

ASK YOURSELF WHAT YOU WANT:

SYMPATHY OR SUCCESS?

VICTORY

Slow growth is good growth,
so you can develop a strong root system
and not topple over in a storm.

I'm not where I want to be,
but thank God I'm not where I used to be.

-THOSE WHO ARE CONSIDERED-
AN OVERNIGHT SUCCESS
WILL TELL YOU
IT WAS ONE LONG NIGHT!

VICTORY

Finishers are simply ordinary people with extraordinary determination.

God is not nearly as interested
in what you have done
as He is in what you are going to do now.

FORGET MOTIVATION.

JUST DO IT!

VICTORY

Yesterday's victory can be
the worst enemy to tomorrow's success.

Many times,
the greatest pressure to quit
comes right before victory.

let the poker of past victories

STIR UP THE COALS OF FUTURE TRIUMPH.

VICTORY

Enjoy the journey
where you presently are,
on the way to where you are going!

Perspective affects attitude,
and attitude affects everything.

REALITY IS WHERE YOU STAND.
VISION IS WHERE YOU SOAR.

VICTORY

Truth believed
will eventually be
truth experienced.

Logic is for order,
but faith is for victory.

EXPECT A

BRIGHTER FUTURE
BY BELIEVING
THE WORD OF GOD
TODAY.

VICTORY

As you overcome, you'll have periods of doing what's right before seeing what's right.

You can change the devil's will. Submit yourself to God, resist the devil, and he *will* flee from you!

WHEN YOU MAGNIFY YOUR GOD,
YOU MINIMIZE YOUR PROBLEMS.

VICTORY

Grace is the power of God
to do what you can't do by yourself.

Change isn't change
until you change.

GOD,
WHO CHANGES NOT, CHANGES US.

VICTORY

Millions will fail because
they are unwilling to change.

Just because you fail
does not mean you are a failure.

LEARN TO FAIL FORWARD

VICTORY

Attitude can be the difference between success and failure.

You are not a failure until you quit.

ATTEMPTING TOO MUCH ALMOST GUARANTEES FAILURE.

VICTORY

When you're established in righteousness,
you know it will be as the Word says.

You may not know where the storm started,
why the storm started,
or who started the storm,
but you can rest your head
on the promises of God
because you're going to the other side!

**LET ADVERSITY
DEEPEN YOUR RESOLVE
FOR VICTORY**

VICTORY

Fear stops you from taking advantage of a God-given opportunity.

Fear is simply courage's opportunity.

FEAR STOPS US from being ALL GOD WANTS US TO BE

VICTORY

Don't run in tough times.
The process that will take you
where you need to go
must be learned right where you are.

When you're drowning,
you can look at it like you are going to die
or see it as an opportunity to learn to swim.

NOTHING LESS THAN TOTAL COMMITMENT WILL GET YOU TO THE PRIZE.

VICTORY

We tend to behold achievers
instead of becoming achievers.
Let's not just look at them;
let's learn from them.

Your greatest hurt can be
someone else's greatest healing.

YOUR AREA OF GREAT ATTACK HAS THE POTENTIAL TO BE A GREAT VICTORY.

VICTORY

It's not what you do when you sin that counts,
but what you do after you sin.

It is important to remove
the mountains in your life
because mountains tend to block
the brightness of your future.

*your today can't change your yesterday.
our today can only change your tomorrow.*

THE MOST IMPORTANT **RELATIONSHIPS IN OUR LIVES ARE BUILT ON** SMALL, CONSISTENT DEPOSITS OF TIME.

FAMILY

FAMILY

It is a mistake to think you have to feel love in order to give love.

When you understand your spouse is not supposed to make you happy, only then can you be happily married.

Working toward a happy marriage is not the same as looking to your marriage for happiness.

FAMILY

Love in marriage is
seeking the highest good
for the other person.

Happy couples trade
a sense of entitlement for
a sense of indebtedness.

THE COMMON INGREDIENT IN ATTRACTION AND AFFECTION IS TIME SPENT TOGETHER.

FAMILY

Pray marriage scriptures over yourself and your spouse daily. They bring faith and reminders to you and power to your spouse.

Trust occurs when words and deeds are congruent.

MUCH LIKE the frame on a beautiful PAINTING trust provides safe boundaries

FAMILY

Learn to let your spouse's differences fascinate you, not irritate you.

Commitment is designed to give your spouse a safe place, knowing that you will stay together even if you are unhappy for a season.

commitment means staying loyal to

WHAT YOU SAID YOU WERE GOING TO DO

long after the mood you said it in

HAS LEFT YOU.

FAMILY

It's not that you and your spouse need to do everything together, but marriage won't work if you are always moving in separate directions.

Sometimes, we are willing to hurt the people we love the most to get what we want the most.

IT'S NOT ALWAYS ABOUT
WHO IS RIGHT,
BUT ABOUT MAKING
THINGS RIGHT.

FAMILY

In seasons of marital difficulty, couples spend less time together to avoid the conflict. But what they think is the solution (avoiding the problem) actually becomes the problem.

Mutual submission is the glue that keeps marriage together. It's frequently asking, from the heart, "What can I do to help?"

HAPPY COUPLES UNDERSTAND THE DIFFERENCE BETWEEN RESOLVING THEIR ANGER AND RESOLVING THEIR ISSUE.

FAMILY

In marriage, there is nothing more vital than clarity and continuance of communication.

Make many sacrifices for your children; just don't sacrifice your marriage.

KIDS ARE CREATED TO LEAVE.
SPOUSES ARE CREATED TO STAY.

FAMILY

If you want your child to believe God's Word, they must see you keeping your word.

Many times, children know *about* Jesus, but they don't *know* Jesus.

TEACH YOUR CHILD TO PUT GOD'S WORD FIRST IN EVERY SITUATION.

FAMILY

Teach your child that
in their difference lies their destiny.

Teach your child that
God has a wonderful plan for their life,
but not a wonderful life for their plan.

teach your child

THE LINK BETWEEN

diligence
AND SUCCESS

FAMILY

Children don't need a cool parent;
they need a consistent parent.

Parents should insulate,
but not isolate.

THE BEST **GIFT** YOU CAN GIVE **YOUR CHILDREN** IS A GREAT MARRIAGE.

FAMILY

Attending your child's sporting event is not quality time.

Being in the same room as your children while you are all on electronic devices is not quality time.

GOOD PARENTING **DOES NOT** HAPPEN ACCIDENTALLY. GOOD PARENTING **HAPPENS** INTENTIONALLY.

FAMILY

If your child has a good heart,
and you just tell them the "what"
without the "why" and "how,"
they will be frustrated.
If you tell them the "what"
with the "why" and "how,"
they will end up motivated.

Fake faith is passed along
just like genuine faith—by example.

Children don't do **WHAT THEY ARE TAUGHT.** *Children do what* **THEY SEE.**

FAMILY

Punishment is something you do to criminals.
Discipline is something you do for children.

Discipline is initially rough, but eventually rewarding.

DISCIPLINE IS AN ACT OF LOVE

FAMILY

If your parenting consists mostly of yelling, you are not setting boundaries and consequences.

Do not rescue your child from consequences.
(Proverbs 19:19)

CONSEQUENCES ARE A TEACHER.

FAMILY

A key to a great marriage is clearly recognizing the differences between men and women.

Happy couples refuse to believe their spouses intended to hurt them. They look for the most generous explanations instead.

doing little things for your spouse will make you happy

FAMILY

Love is not a feeling; love is a choice.
Choices lead. Feelings follow.

Isn't it funny how
we'll love unconditionally
as long as people are
meeting our conditions?

COMMITMENT COMES FROM CHOICES, NOT CONDITIONS.

FAMILY

A woman saying "thank you" to her husband is the emotional equivalent of a man saying "I love you" to his wife.

Learn to accept and appreciate your mate.

WHAT YOU ARE THANKFUL FOR
WILL ALWAYS STAY FRESH IN YOUR LIFE.

ASSOCIATION GIVES YOU MOTIVATION FOR YOUR DESTINATION.

FRIENDS

FRIENDS

Relationships become bad when
nothing is done to make them good.
Relationships are good because
the effort was made to make them good.

Good relationships are possible,
but not probable.
Good relationships are impossible
when we follow the culture.

RELATIONSHIPS ARE LIKE BANK ACCOUNTS. IN ORDER TO WITHDRAW FROM THEM, YOU MUST INVEST IN THEM ON A REGULAR BASIS.

FRIENDS

Always leave a light at the end
of everybody's tunnel.

Be the one who gives pats on the back,
not someone who is looking for them.

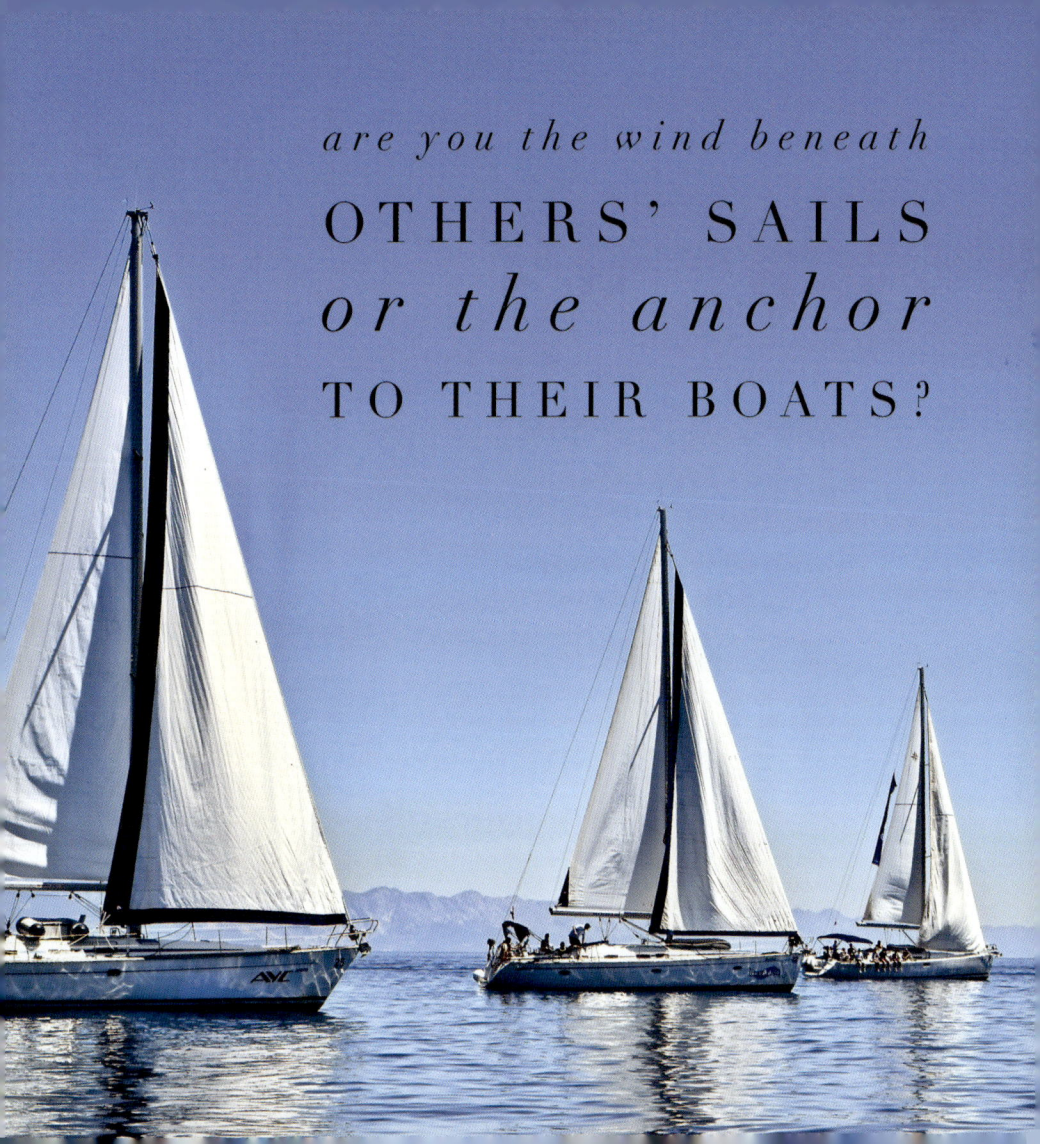

are you the wind beneath
OTHERS' SAILS
or the anchor
TO THEIR BOATS?

FRIENDS

Always extend the hand of mercy
before you point the finger of judgment.

Show pity to everyone
but yourself.

Being kind doesn't mean you never raise your voice. Being kind means you never raise your temper.

FRIENDS

When you love someone,
they become desirable.
When you respect someone,
they become valuable.

Never spend more time answering a critic
than you would assisting a friend.

CHARACTER
{ IS THE }
FOUNDATION OF
RESPECT.

FRIENDS

Devaluing others never makes you more valuable.

Your relationship with someone begins to decline the moment you take them for granted.

YOUR BLOWING OUT ANOTHER MAN'S CANDLE NEVER MAKES YOURS SHINE ANY BRIGHTER

FRIENDS

If you can't trust a person in all points,
you can't trust a person in any point.

Trust is an issue of character.
Respect is an issue of competence.
Many times, we trust people we don't respect.

IT'S EASY TO TRUST THOSE WHO TRULY LOVE YOU

FRIENDS

If you go somewhere to find a friend,
you won't find them anywhere.
If you go somewhere to be a friend,
you will find them everywhere.

We tend to put down in others
what we put up with in ourselves.

WHEN HE GETS THE CHANCE,
A GOOD LEADER MAKES A FRIEND.

FRIENDS

God will place you with those who are similar so that when they rub you the wrong way, you notice just how abrasive *you* can be!

You can hurt others from a place of moral superiority or hypocrisy.

— PEOPLE —
ARE THE "SANDPAPER OF GOD" TO RUB OFF YOUR ROUGH SPOTS.

FRIENDS

Technology is all about information.
Relationships are all about communication.

Unity doesn't take away your individuality;
it just means you'll have to
get along with different personalities.

Love people and use things, not the other way around.

FRIENDS

It's not just about what is said,
but also about how it is said.

You have not communicated
until someone understands.

IN ORDER TO BE **A GOOD** COMMUNICATOR, YOU NEED TO BE A GOOD LISTENER.

FRIENDS

You don't truly know someone until you disagree with them.

Conflict reveals character.

LEARN TO DISAGREE
agreeably.

FRIENDS

Learning to accept others' limitations is a key to successful, long-term relationships.

Find the oak tree in every acorn and praise it.

LOVE PEOPLE FOR WHO THEY ARE, *not* WHO THEY AREN'T.

FRIENDS

If you compromise to keep a relationship, eventually you won't recognize yourself.

Never hand the reins of your emotional well-being to another person.
They will always steer you in the wrong direction.

FEELINGS ARE NOT ALWAYS RIGHT,
but they are always real.

FRIENDS

Your vulnerable relationships
are your valuable relationships.

Learn to associate with those
who help you see your objectives,
not just your obstacles.

LEARN TO ASSOCIATE WITH THOSE WHO ARE MORE EXCITED ABOUT YOUR FUTURE THAN THEY ARE ABOUT YOUR PAST.

FRIENDS

God operates through representation.

You don't have to go through
a representative to get to God,
but God will go through
a representative to get to you.

TO GET WHAT GOD INTENDS, YOU MUST RECEIVE WHOM GOD SENDS

WE CHOOSE OUR LIVES

BY HOW WE SPEND

OUR TIME AND MONEY.

FINANCES

FINANCES

The answer is not new money,
but a new way of thinking about money.

Faithfulness is revealed in fruitfulness.
Fruitfulness is revealed in production.

PRODUCTIVITY PROMOTES PROSPERITY.

FINANCES

Don't be a consumer.
Be a producer.

A rich person who is stingy
is just a poor person with money.

IF MONEY IS A MYSTERY TO YOU, MONEY WILL BE MISSING FROM YOU.

FINANCES

Money is not moral or immoral.
Money is amoral.
It's what you do with money
that determines morality.

Prosperity and poverty begin in the heart
and eventually show up in your life.

MONEY DOESN'T CREATE CHARACTER.

MONEY REVEALS CHARACTER.

FINANCES

You don't need more money to live on;
you need something to live for.

Contentment causes you to
enjoy your today.
Desire causes you to
expect a better tomorrow.

Focus on what you do have, not what you don't have.

FINANCES

It's all right to desire more,
just don't forget to enjoy
where you are right now.

Never buy stuff with
money that you don't have
to impress someone that you don't like.

**THERE IS A DIFFERENCE BETWEEN QUALITY OF LIFE
AND STANDARD OF LIVING.**

FINANCES

If you don't hate debt,
you'll tolerate it.

Your bad financial habit
will eventually become
someone else's
financial problem.

IF YOUR OUTGO

IS MORE THAN YOUR INCOME,

THEN YOUR UPKEEP
WILL BE YOUR DOWNFALL.

FINANCES

Abundance does not come overnight.
Abundance comes over time.

Never follow things.
Follow God, and let things follow you.

OPTIONS COME WITH MONEY. IF YOU CAN HANDLE THE OPTIONS, GOD WILL GIVE YOU THE MONEY.

FINANCES

God doesn't want to just raise
your standard of living;
He wants to raise
your standard of giving.

The value of your life is not defined by
how much you have accumulated.
The value of your life is defined by
how much you give away.

TRUST GOD WITH 10%,
AND HE WILL BECOME YOUR FINANCIAL ADVISOR FOR THE OTHER 90%.

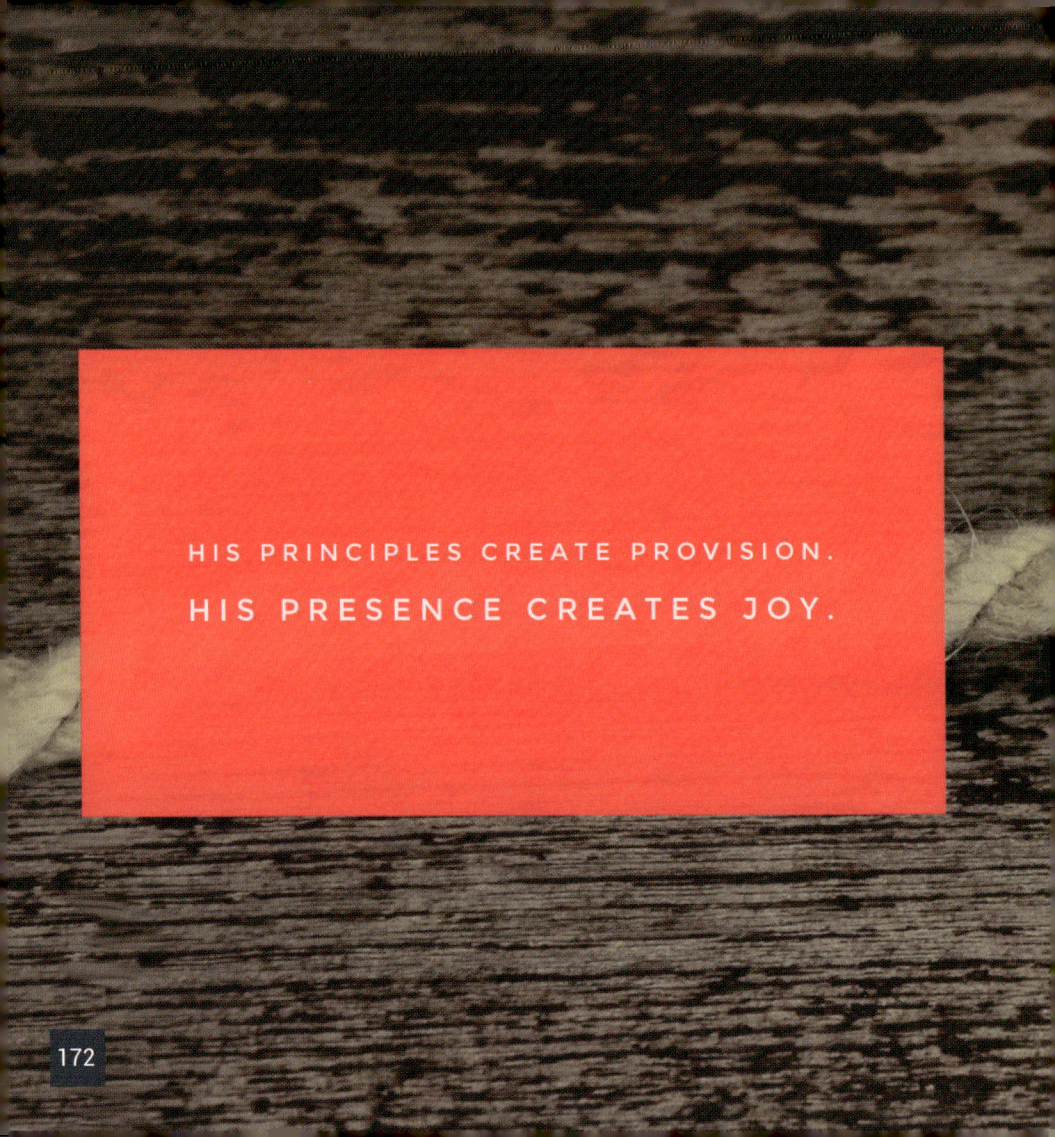

HIS PRINCIPLES CREATE PROVISION.
HIS PRESENCE CREATES JOY.

GOD'S LOVE

GOD'S LOVE

God loves you as much as He loves Jesus.
(John 17:23)

Let how God sees you define you.

you're accepted **BY THE BEST.** *who cares* ABOUT THE REST?

GOD'S LOVE

God loves you in spite of what you do,
not because of what you do.

Quit trying to satisfy
an already-satisfied God.

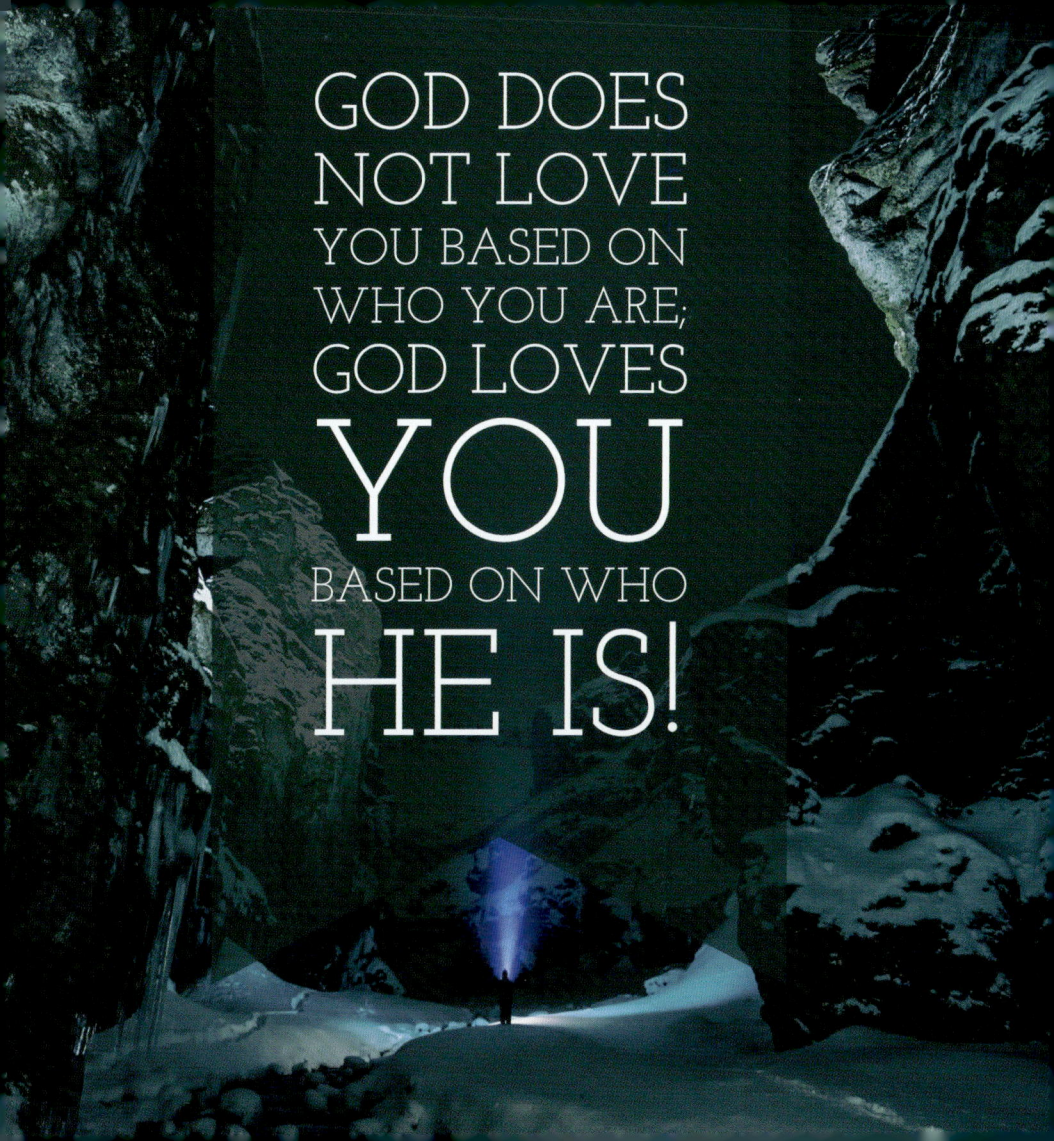

GOD DOES NOT LOVE YOU BASED ON WHO YOU ARE; GOD LOVES **YOU** BASED ON WHO **HE IS!**

GOD'S LOVE

God's love is never based
on the character of the receiver.
God's love is based on
the character of the Giver.

God doesn't just have love—He is love.

understanding his passion

FOR YOU
will ignite
YOUR PASSION
FOR HIM.

GOD'S LOVE

When God's Word becomes
the main part of your prayer life,
you start with the solution
instead of the problem.

Whenever you go to God in prayer,
never go based on what
you have or haven't done.
Always go to God based on what
He has done for you.

PRAYER IS NOT JUST FOR COMFORT, BUT FOR RESULTS!

GOD'S LOVE

God is not a car-wrecking, cancer-causing Creator, but a loving, life-giving Lord.

God wants you to have abundant life, provision, health, relationships, fruitfulness, and joy.

BIG OR SMALL, *God Cares* ABOUT IT ALL!

GOD'S LOVE

His greatness encourages us to revere Him, but His goodness encourages us to approach Him.

There is never a time that you come into the presence of God and He doesn't give you something.

YOU ARE ALWAYS *comfortable in the* PRESENCE OF THOSE

WHO LOVE YOU

GOD'S LOVE

Your pile of sins is never bigger
than the pile of God's mercy.

Forget your sin,
but remember that you have been forgiven.

GOD HAS A PLAN FOR WHEREVER YOU LAND.

GOD LOVES YOU

AS IF YOU WERE
THE ONLY
PERSON
IN THIS WORLD
TO LOVE

HOW TO START THE MOST IMPORTANT RELATIONSHIP OF YOUR LIFE

Shark fishing is my hobby. I use a kayak to paddle my bait hundreds of yards into the ocean, then paddle back and fish from the shore. Some time ago, I was in the midst of a four-hour battle with a very large shark. A crowd had gathered from around the beach to see what I was going to reel in! A man in the crowd struck up a conversation with me while I was battling this shark. He asked me what I did for a living, and I told him I was a pastor. When people discover that I am a pastor, I get a wide variety of responses.

This man's response was unusual. He simply blurted out with disdain, "Well, I hate organized religion!" You could visibly tell that he was not expecting my response. "Me too," I replied. He was very surprised, so I continued. I asked, "You know who else hates organized religion?" Before he could respond, I shocked him further and said, "Jesus!" Now I had this fellow's undivided attention, and I hope I now have yours as well.

You see, Christianity is not about religion. It is about a relationship with a loving, heavenly Father through His one Son, Jesus Christ. I believe you have a figurative homing beacon placed on the inside of you by the One who created you: God. A spiritual hole, if you will, that can only be filled by God.

I understand this personally. Before I entered into a relationship with Jesus, I tried to fill that hole with women, alcohol, and fighting. It was fun for a while, but when the fun was over, and the things I tried to fill that vacuum with came crashing down around me, I still had that homing beacon on the inside of me. My heavenly Father gently, patiently, and ever so lovingly calling me home.

Maybe you can sense the emptiness on the inside of you and the loving call of your heavenly Father, imploring you to come home. Why not surrender your life to Him and find the joy, peace, and purpose you've been looking for all of your life? Why not start the most important relationship of your life? It's so simple, but life transforming.

Please pray this prayer with me. Repeat it out loud, but mean it from your heart. I discovered a long time ago that when you reach out to God from your heart, He will always reach back to you with His love.

Pray this simple prayer with me now:

"Father God, I come to you now. Sin, I turn my back on you. Jesus, I turn to You now. I believe you died on the cross just for me. I believe you were raised from the dead just for me. Come into my heart, and be my Lord. I surrender my life to you today. I enter into relationship with you today!"

If you prayed that prayer, please contact us here at Joy Church, and let us know that you started the most important relationship of your life. We want to respect your privacy and dignity, but we also want to give you some information to help you walk out this new relationship in a life-giving way!

You can email us at mail@joychurchinternational.org or give us a call at 615-773-5252. You can write to us at Joy Church, P.O. Box 247, Mount Juliet, TN, 37121.

If you live in or are visiting the Nashville/Mount Juliet, TN area, we would love to invite you to join us for one of our upcoming services. For more information and directions, please visit our website at www.joychurch.net. We look forward to hearing from you!

Please remember that God loves you as if you were the only person in this world to love!

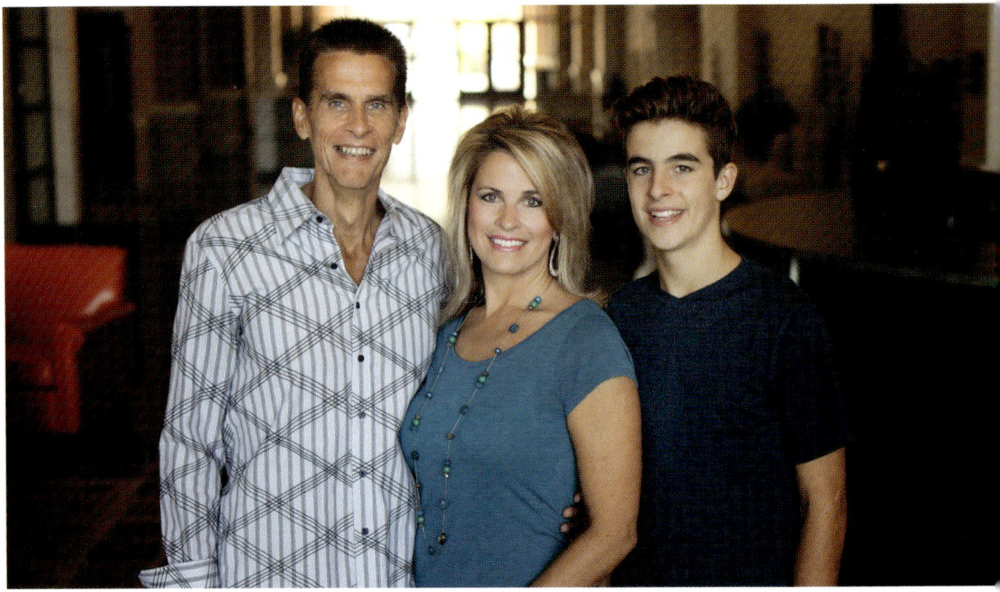

ABOUT THE AUTHOR

Jim Frease is the founder and Senior Pastor of Joy Church in Mount Juliet, Tennessee, and founder and President of World Changers Bible Institute (WCBI). He is also the founder of Joy Ministerial Exchange (JME), a ministerial organization designed to impart to pastors from across the country.

Jim emphasizes a relationship with Jesus Christ, not religion; the Word of God, not tradition; and he emphasizes enjoying one's life, not enduring it. He teaches not just what to do, but how.

Jim and his wife Anne have been married since 1990 and deeply love their son, Johnathan. Jim loves spending time with his family, and enjoys Ohio State football, fishing, Ohio State football, fishing, and Ohio State football. Anne loves to shop. Sometimes, they compromise and shop at Bass Pro.

Most importantly, Jim and Anne are deeply in love with the Lord Jesus Christ and are completely committed to His Word. As they minister, they do so with humor, joy (Nehemiah 8:10) and integrity (Psalm 26:11), propelling the listener to a greater intimacy with Jesus.

JOY
church
Tired of enduring life? Start enjoying life!

Based out of Mt. Juliet, Tennessee, Joy Church is a rapidly growing, multi-generational, multicultural church with people from almost every denominational background—including those with no church background at all.

At Joy Church, we don't believe in organized religion; we believe in organized *relationship* with God the Father through His Son, Jesus Christ. We are not about tradition, but the liberating Word of God. We are not about enduring life—we are about *enjoying* life!

For more information, please visit us online at www.joychurch.net.

WINNING WITH WISDOM

PEARLS OF WISDOM FOR YOUR NEXT RIGHT DECISION